Cut!

How Lotte Reiniger and a Pair of Scissors
Revolutionized Animation

WRITTEN BY
C. E. WINTERS & MATT SCHU

ILLUSTRATED BY
MATT SCHU

Greenwillow Books, *An Imprint of HarperCollinsPublishers*

Cut!: How Lotte Reiniger and a Pair of Scissors Revolutionized Animation
Text copyright © 2023 by C. E. Winters
Illustrations copyright © 2023 by Matt Schu
All rights reserved. Manufactured in Italy.
For information address HarperCollins Children's Books, a division of
HarperCollins Publishers, 195 Broadway, New York, NY 10007.
www.harpercollinschildrens.com

The full-color art was created digitally using Photoshop and Procreate® for iPad.
The text type is Venetian 301 BT Demi.

Library of Congress Cataloging-in-Publication Data is available.

ISBN 978-0-06-306739-4 (hardcover)

23 24 25 26 27 RTLO 10 9 8 7 6 5 4 3 2 1
First Edition

Greenwillow Books

For Meggie and Erin—C. E. W.

For my family—M. S.

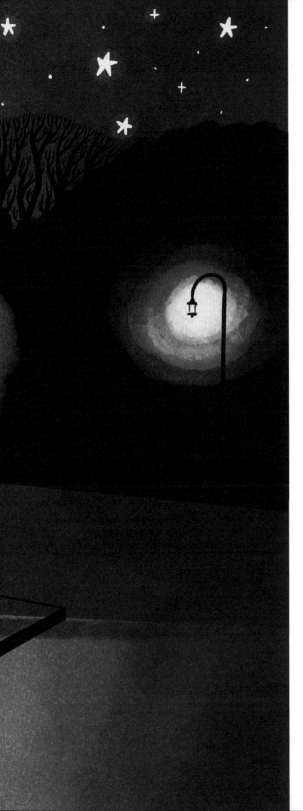

W hen Lotte was little, movies were new.

Her grandmother took her to the theaters of Berlin, Germany. They watched movies that were silent but filled with magical sights.

Up on the screen, characters vanished in puffs of smoke. Villains changed their appearance in the blink of an eye. Objects and scenery moved about as though alive.

I want to make this type of magic, thought Lotte.

But she didn't know anything about making movies.

What Lotte did know *plenty* about was a form of art called Scherenschnitte, a German word meaning "scissor cuts." She would pick up a pair of scissors and . . .

snip, snip, snip!

She cut characters out of paper. Silhouettes.

She decided to bring her paper figures to life and use them to tell stories, as if she was a filmmaker. She cut out different sections of a character's body and connected the pieces using wire, creating bendable joints, like elbows and knees. She could then make her figures move.

Lotte built her own puppet theater, and she and her silhouette characters entertained her classmates and teachers with performances of *Romeo and Juliet* and other plays by William Shakespeare.

But she dreamed of entertaining much larger audiences.

When Lotte grew a little older, she went to a theater and heard a famous actor and director, Paul Wegener, give a speech. He explained the importance of the camera in moviemaking and said he used mirrors and other tricks to change what audiences saw onscreen. He talked about animation and movie magic.

Lotte rushed home and asked her parents if she could attend the acting school where Paul Wegener taught, so she might one day make movies with him.

Eventually they said yes.

Even at acting school, Lotte
carried around a pair of scissors and
paper. While waiting backstage for her
chance to perform, she snapped open her
scissors.

She cut out silhouettes of the actors
striking dramatic poses onstage. She showed
her artwork to Mr. Wegener, hoping he would
see that she was talented enough to make movies.

Soon enough, her plan worked. Mr. Wegener asked Lotte to cut words and pictures out of paper to appear between scenes and help tell the stories in his silent films. Lotte became a part of his moviemaking team.

But she wanted to learn and do more.

Next Mr. Wegener taught Lotte about stop-motion animation, a camera trick that made objects look like they were moving.

In an old German village, Lotte placed fake wooden rats on a cobblestone street. She hid in a cellar while a camera operator took a picture of the rats. Then she crawled back out to nudge the little rodents a fraction of an inch forward.

She hid again.

The camera captured another picture.

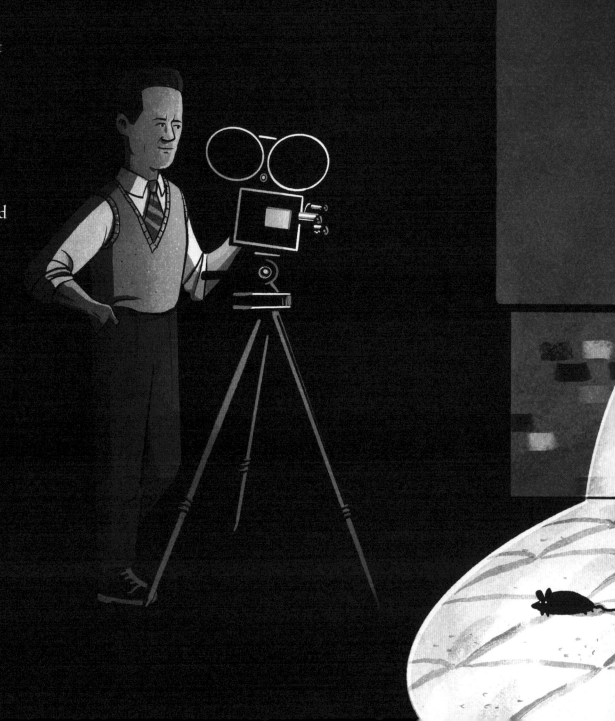

Lotte repeated this process over and over for hours.

Move, stop. Move, stop.

In the finished film, all those pictures of the rats flowed together and created the illusion of movement on the screen. The wooden rats appeared to scamper across the road just like real rats.

Movie magic!

Paul Wegener also introduced Lotte to a
group of artists and filmmakers at the Institute
for Cultural Research, a Berlin studio that
produced movies and animations that looked
new and different.

snip,

snip,

snip!

With the help of other members of the studio, Lotte designed and directed one of the world's first animated silhouette movies: *The Ornament of the Loving Heart*, a four-minute love story with dancing shadows.

snip,
snip,
snip!

Audiences loved *The Ornament of the Loving Heart* so much that Lotte got the chance to make more short films at the studio—films inspired by fairy tales and legends. Other studios invited her to create silhouette scenes for their movies. Publishers asked her to illustrate books.

During the same time, Lotte fell in love with her camera operator, Carl Koch, who was also a filmmaker and an art historian. The couple soon married.

One day, a banker and supporter of the arts named Louis Hagen observed Lotte working in the studio. He asked, "Would you do a full-length silhouette film?"

"I don't think one can do that," said Lotte. "Animated films are supposed to make people roar with laughter, and nobody has dared entertain an audience with them for more than ten minutes."

"Well, I would be interested," said Mr. Hagen, and he gave Lotte enough film to create a movie that would run well over an hour long. He also offered her a room at his home to use as a studio.

Despite her doubts, Lotte was inspired to meet this giant animation challenge. She gathered a small team of animators, including her husband, and traveled to the studio at Mr. Hagen's house. She sketched and mapped out ideas.

Lotte cut silhouette characters and scenery from sheets of lead and black cardboard.

She planned to place her silhouettes on a sheet of glass over a special table called her Tricktisch—her trick table.

Light bulbs would shine up through the glass and turn her designs into shadow and light. A camera would point down at her silhouettes.

But Lotte worried that her scenes might look too flat, like drawings in a book. For a movie this major, she wanted to give her animations the illusion of depth—as though some things were close and others far away.

To solve the problem, Lotte designed a wooden tower that allowed the camera to gaze down on her table from several feet above. She built the structure so it could hold multiple layers of glass.

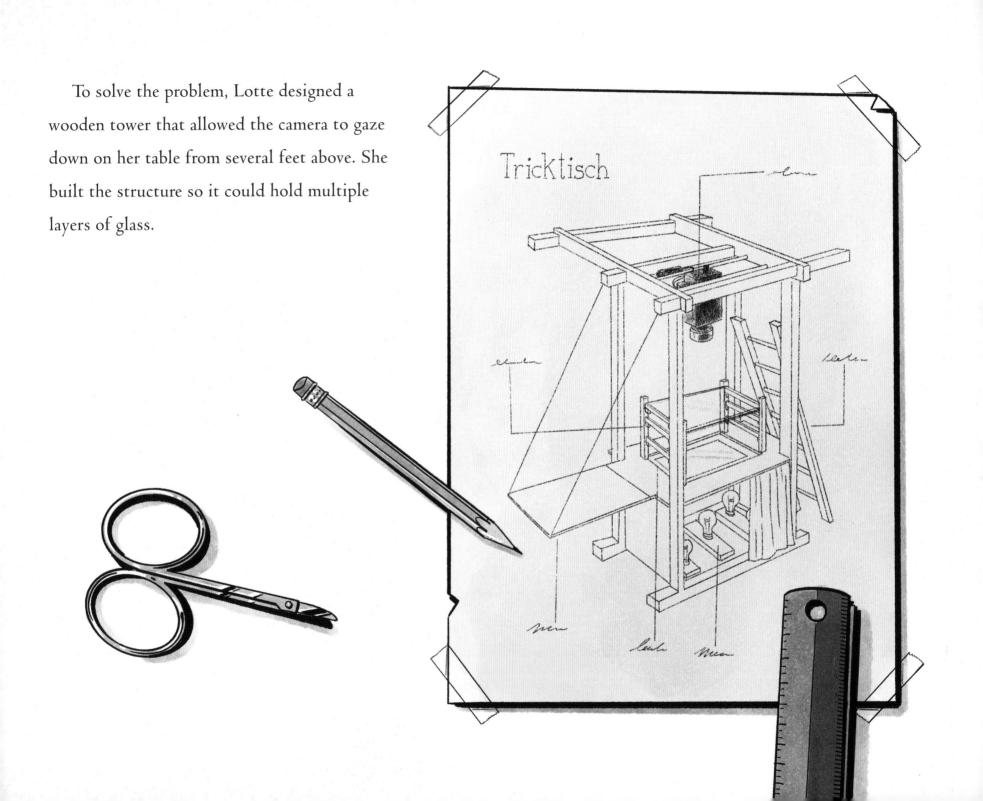

Tricktisch

She positioned her silhouette characters on an upper sheet of glass,
while one of her team members set up backgrounds on a lower sheet.
When everything looked just right, a team member took a picture.

Lotte then moved her characters a fraction of an inch on their layer of glass, just as she had done with the wooden rats. But the background scenery stayed the same.

The camera captured another picture.

Move, stop. Move, stop.

In the finished scenes, her characters appeared to be closer to the audience than the distant background art. And if Lotte placed scenery on upper layers of glass and characters on lower ones, the scenery looked closer.

Her silhouette figures performed in a fantastical three-dimensional world. Lotte had invented the multiplane camera.

Lotte spent nearly three long years making her full-length animated film.

But when it was finished, theaters refused to show it.

"No one wants to see an hour-long cartoon!" said theater owners. Lotte and her team had been working on their film quietly, without any publicity, so the theaters also said, "We don't know who you are."

With the help of a friend, Lotte found an out-of-the-way theater in the north of Berlin that agreed to show her movie.

Ihr seid eingeladen zur Uraufführung von "Die Abenteuer des *Prinzen Achmed!*"

Lotte and Carl wrote out 8,000 invitations by hand, asking people to come see her one-of-a-kind film.

On a Sunday morning in May 1926, a large, curious crowd piled into the theater. Live orchestra music rose into the air. A movie projector clicked and whirred in the shadows.

Lotte's new movie, *The Adventures of Prince Achmed*, flickered to life across the screen.

For sixty-five breathtaking minutes, the audience fell under the spell of Lotte's creation.

They applauded her work throughout the entire film.

The Adventures of Prince Achmed dazzled people so much that it traveled to theaters in France, England, Japan, and eventually the United States.

"She has fairy hands," audiences said of Lotte as they exited the doors at the film's French premiere.

The young woman with lightning-quick fingers and a mind dancing with ideas proved that—*yes!*—people *were* willing to watch animated movies for much longer than ten minutes.

Lotte would make approximately sixty silhouette films over the course of her long life. She even made some of them while fleeing across Europe before and during World War II. When she and Carl returned to Germany to care for Lotte's sick mother, she made a film during the bombing of Berlin, while hiding in a basement. She made others for the brand-new world of television after she moved to the calm and safety of England.

She created every single one of those films using a pair of scissors, a great deal of patience, and her talented hands. Her trailblazing ideas and silhouette style influence filmmakers and artists to this day.

snip!
snip!
snip!

THE END!

Snippets of Lotte Reiniger's Life

June 2, 1899 Charlotte (Lotte) Reiniger is born in Charlottenburg, Germany (now part of Berlin).

1916 Lotte enrolls in Max Reinhardt's theater school in Berlin. She designs silhouettes for Paul Wegener's movie *Rübezahls Hochzeit (Rübezahl's Marriage)*.

1918 Lotte helps create an animated sequence for Wegener's movie *Der Rattenfänger von Hameln (The Pied Piper of Hamelin)*.

1919 Lotte joins the Institut für Kulturforschung (Institute for Cultural Research), a studio that makes experimental animations and educational films.

December 12, 1919 Lotte releases her first film, *Das Ornament des verliebten Herzens (The Ornament of the Loving Heart)*.

1921 Lotte marries filmmaker Carl Koch.

1923 Louis Hagen gives Lotte a large quantity of film, a studio, and money that allows her to make a full-length animated movie.

1923–1926 Using more than 250,000 silhouette images, Lotte and her team make *Die Abenteuer des Prinzen Achmed (The Adventures of Prince Achmed)* in Potsdam, Germany. Lotte designs a multiplane camera. The invention will improve the way animations are filmed for years to come.

May 2, 1926 *The Adventures of Prince Achmed* debuts at the Volksbühne, a Berlin theater.

1935 Lotte and Carl flee Germany after Adolf Hitler and his Nazi Party take control of the country. Lotte continues to make her films across Europe.

September 1, 1939 World War II begins in Europe.

1943 Lotte and Carl return to Germany to take care of Lotte's sick mother.

1944 Lotte makes the short film *Die Goldene Gans (The Golden Goose)* while hiding in a basement during the bombing of Berlin.

May 8, 1945 Germany surrenders, and World War II ends in Europe.

1949 Lotte and Carl move to London.

1952 Lotte and Carl form Primrose Productions with Louis Hagen Jr., the son of the banker who provided the film and money to make *The Adventures of Prince Achmed*. Lotte creates silhouette animations for a new generation of viewers through television.

1963 Carl passes away.

1970 Lotte publishes the book *Shadow Theatres and Shadow Films* and teaches others how to make silhouettes that move.

June 19, 1981 Lotte passes away in Germany just after her eighty-second birthday, after designing and directing approximately sixty silhouette films.

Author's Note

When she first picked up a pair of scissors and created her silhouettes, Lotte Reiniger drew upon a long multicultural history of paper art and shadow plays. Artistic paper cutting originated in China and eventually traveled to countries around the world, including Lotte's home country of Germany, where the art form became known as Scherenschnitte.

Lotte developed her love of shadow puppetry as a child in the early 1900s and carried that passion through her entire filmmaking career. She was known for her lightning-quick, highly detailed cutting skills.

Many of Lotte's filmmaking accomplishments—the oldest surviving full-length animated film, the first multiplane camera, the invention of a process called storyboarding that involved sketching and mapping out ideas for a film—have been credited to a more well-known figure in animation history: Walt Disney. Film historians agree that Disney didn't steal or necessarily even know about Lotte's work and inventions, but Disney's animation achievements in 1930s America have received far more attention than Lotte's achievements in 1920s Germany. Several of her films were lost or destroyed, which also caused people to overlook her career.

My hope in writing this book is to bring Lotte Reiniger out from the shadows of history, to set the record straight about her contributions to the field of animation, and to inspire young artists and inventors to let their imaginations soar well beyond traditional limits—just as Lotte did.

You can still find the influence of Lotte's silhouettes in modern-day movies, TV series, and illustrations, and on the covers of numerous books.

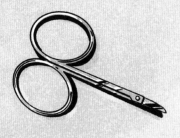

Sources

Books and Articles

Blattner, Evamarie, and Karlheinz Wiegmann, eds. *Lotte Reiniger: "Mit zaubernden Händen geboren": Drei Scherenschnittfolgen* (in English: *Lotte Reiniger: "Born with Enchanting Hands": Three Silhouette Sequels.*) Berlin: Wasmuth, 2012.

Grace, Whitney. *Lotte Reiniger: Pioneer of Film Animation.* Jefferson, NC: McFarland & Company, 2017.

Guerin, Frances, and Anke Mebold. "Lotte Reiniger." In *Women Film Pioneers Project,* edited by Jane Gaines, Radha Vatsal, and Monica Dall'Asta. Center for Digital Research and Scholarship. New York, NY: Columbia University Libraries, 2013. Web, July 6, 2016. https://doi.org/10.7916/d8-6m3p-mh27

Reiniger, Lotte. "Scissors Make Films." *Sight and Sound*, Spring 1936. https://www2.bfi.org.uk/news-opinion/sight-sound-magazine/archives/lotte-reiniger-scissors-make-films-cut-out-animation-process-description-1936

Reiniger, Lotte. *Shadow Theatres and Shadow Films.* London, England: B. T. Batsford Ltd., 1970.

Audio Recording

Reiniger, Lotte. "Lotte Reiniger Recording," 1976. Kenneth Clouse Collection, Hugh M. Hefner Moving Image Archive, University of Southern California School of Cinematic Arts. http://www.uschefnerarchive.com/project/lotte-reiniger-recording/

Documentaries

The Art of Lotte Reiniger, directed by John Isaacs. Primrose Productions, 1970.

Lotte Reiniger: Homage to the Inventor of the Silhouette Film, directed by Katja Raganelli. Bayerischer Rundfunk and Diorama Film Munich GmbH, 1999.

Lotte Reiniger im Stadtmuseum Tübingen, Universitätsstadt Tübingen, 2015.

Lotte That Silhouette Girl, directed by Elizabeth Beech and Carla Patullo. Trick Studio, 2018.

Glossary of German Words & Phrases

Dornröschen: *Sleeping Beauty*

Ihr seid eingeladen zur Uraufführung von "Die Abenteuer des Prinzen Achmed": You are invited to the premiere of *The Adventures of Prince Achmed*

Scherenschnitte: scissor cuts

Tricktisch: trick table